Mummy Took
Cooking Lessons

and Other Poems

by JOHN CIARDI

Illustrated by Merle Nacht

HOUGHTON MIFFLIN COMPANY

BOSTON 1990

Library of Congress Cataloging-in-Publication Data

Ciardi, John, 1916–1986
    Mummy took cooking lessons and other poems / by John Ciardi;
illustrated by Merle Nacht.
        p. cm.
    Summary: A collection of thirty-one poems, many of them humorous.
    ISBN 0-395-53351-1
    1. Children's poetry, American. [1. American poetry.
2. Humorous poetry.] I. Nacht, Merle, ill. II. Title.
PS3505.I27M8   1990   90-4049
811'.52—dc20   CIP
                           AC

Printed in the United States of America

BP 10 9 8 7 6 5 4 3 2 1

FOREWORD

Shortly after John Ciardi's death on Easter day, 1986, I was asked by his family to serve as literary executor of the estate — a title without legal definition but long established in practice and clearly understood to designate the person who brings some kind of order out of the chaos of paper left behind by a deceased writer. I consequently spent many hours over a period of months, running far past the next Easter season, at the Ciardi homes in New Jersey and Key West, reading, identifying, sorting, and trying to evaluate the writing I found in cabinets and desks and boxes, folded in books, and scribbled on the backs of old letters.

Among the work discovered were John's World War II journal, essays and talks, and baskets of poetry. I brought the poems home to Fayetteville, where I began to separate out what seemed to me the most compelling, the clearly finished pieces. I was helped in this by the years John and I had sent the various drafts of our poems back and forth to one another, scribbling suggestions and questions. I was aided as much (because for John to have a poem finished did not necessarily mean having it typed) by the patience, dedication, and intuition of Betty Williams (no relation), one of the editors at the University of Arkansas Press, who spent most all her working days for half a year deciphering John's handwriting until she began to wonder if she would be able again to read ordinary penmanship.

Then she typed, and I read, and we double-checked and read again.

When we had gathered and culled, we prepared what we believed to be two excellent collections — only a small fraction, even so, of the work left. One of the collections — the poems for adults — Arkansas published as *Echoes: Poems Left Behind*. The first printing sold out in six weeks; it has received excellent reviews and is presently in its third printing.

The other collection — the poems for children — we forwarded to Houghton Mifflin. More culling took place in Boston, and you know the rest.

I'm sure that *Mummy Took Cooking Lessons* will be as successful as *Echoes*, because John brought to the children's poems the same skill and understanding with which he approached the writing of his poems for grown-ups, and perhaps more love.

— Miller Williams
    Director, University of Arkansas Press

CONTENTS

Mummy Took Cooking Lessons

Mummy Took Cooking Lessons and . . .

There's this to be said for Mummy's bread:
   It weighs a pound to the ounce.
And if you drop it on the floor
   It certainly does bounce.

Another thing is — it lasts and lasts.
   It starts too hard to harden.
It's tough to chew, but it should do
   For starting a rock garden.

Did I say hard to chew? Well, yes,
   I think it might be — but
I must confess that's just a guess.
   It's much too hard to cut.

And it won't break. I tried the sledge,
   It broke the handle in two.
So, as I say, her bread just *may*
   Be a little hard to chew.

But I don't know for certain,
   And it really wouldn't be just
To claim I *knew* it is hard to chew —
   Not till I break the crust.

In Copenhagen by the Sea

In Copenhagen by the sea
   The seamen go ashore
For a cup or two of sassafras tea
   At the sassafras teacup store.

They munch a cookie, and then they go
   To sing in the village choir.
And some sing high, and some sing low
   And some sing lower and higher.

Hi

"Hi," said Billy. "Hi," said the cook.
  "Nice day," said Billy. "It is," said she.
"Busy?" "I haven't had time to look.
  I've been baking since half past three."

"Anything special?" "Oh, just some cake,
  And cookies, and candy, and pies, and such."
"You didn't happen by some mistake
  To bake a little bit too much?"

"Well, no. About the right amount —
  Five cakes, ten pies, and then I guess
A thousand cookies — by a very rough count —
  Say a thousand more or less."

"You don't suppose it might be more
  By maybe one or two or three?"
"Well, yes. It *could* be as much as four."
  "Could there be one in there for me?"

"I'm just not sure. But look by the sink.
  Do you see a little pie
That's marked with a B? It was baked, I think,
  Just in case you happened by."

Betty Bopper

This is Little Betty Bopper.
She has popcorn in the popper.
Seven pounds of it! Please stop her.
That's more popcorn than is proper
In a popper. Someone drop her
Just a hint! Mommer! Popper!
Betty's going to come a cropper!
Look, it's starting! Get a chopper.
Chop the door down!

            . . . Well, too late.

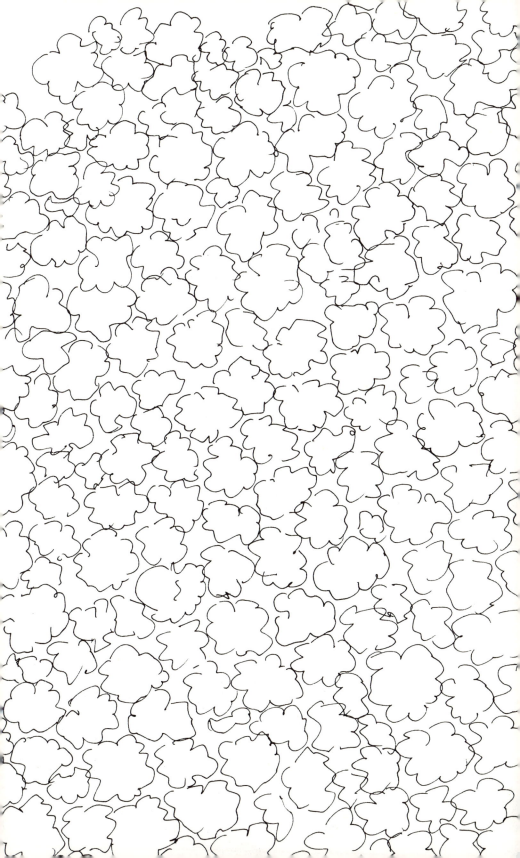

The Milkman Comes at Four
in the Morning

The milkman came at four o'clock.
   The moon was in a dream.
The old dog barked a year ago
   To beg a pint of cream.

The milkman came another night.
   The moon was on his shoulder.
He left the cream the old dog licked,
   And now it's one year older.

The milkman comes, the milkman goes,
   And year by year by year
The moon comes up, the moon goes down.
   The old dog isn't here.

The milkman used to drive a horse.
   Now it's a Chevrolet.
The old dog barked, then went to sleep
   And slept itself away.

Lemonade for Sale

Cut the lemon through the peel.
    The juice is all inside.
When you squeeze it (if it squirts)
    You must step aside.

Lemon squirt can make you smart
    If it hits your eye.
Well, it might not work for you.
    You won't know till you try.

Sugar in the sugar tin.
    Water in the tap.
Fill the pitcher to the brim.
    Hold it in your lap.

When it's full enough you'll feel
    Water down your shin.
That's the time to put a hundred
    Ice cubes in.

Who?

Who is my very best almost friend?
I'll start by saying, "Not you."
The End

The Boy Who Knew He Was Good

There once was a boy who knew he was good.
　　He knew it and knew it and knew it.
Whenever he had some work to do
　　He would do it and do it and do it.

When he had done and done and done
　　And someone said, "Let's play,"
He would say, "There is work to do.
　　Go away. Go away. Go away."

He'd look all day and he'd look all night
　　For something that had to be done.
He worked so hard just looking for work,
　　That even before he'd begun,

He was tired, and weak, and out of breath,
　　But he did what he had to do.
He did it and did it and did it and did it
　　And did it, and when he was through,

He would look all night and look all day
　　For something that had to be done.
He was a worker, a worker, a worker,
　　But when did he have any fun?

Do You Suppose?

Twice a day at twelve o'clock
Two little men run round my block,
One at midnight, one at noon.
If they keep it up, how soon
Do you suppose they'll ever meet
One another on the street?

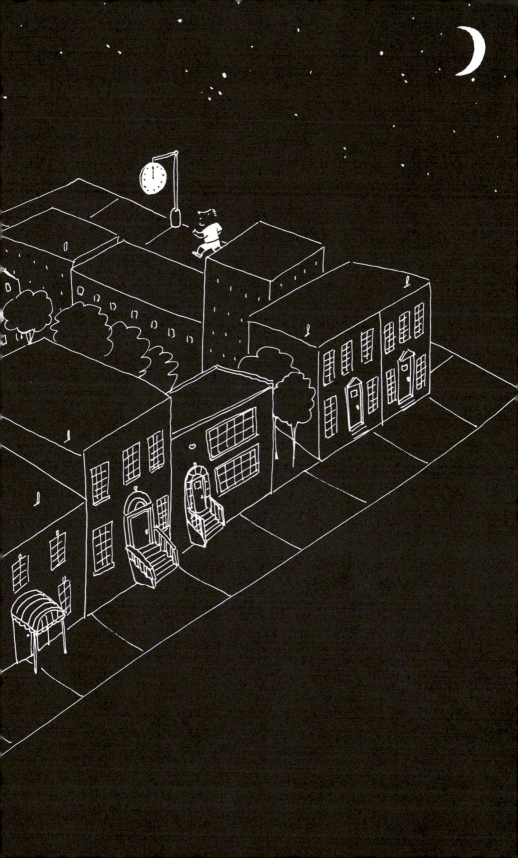

Dirty Dan Ploof

Dirty Dan Ploof was the terror of Yuma.
He rode into town on a ten-foot puma.
He wore a cannon on his hip.
He cracked a rattlesnake for a whip.
He ate two crocodiles every meal
And washed them down with molten steel
Sprinkled with pieces of old barbed wire.
When he breathed out, the town caught fire.
He smothered the flames with his dirty beard
While the church choir sang and the town
    drunks cheered.
"Nothing to it," said Dirty Dan Ploof,
"When you're dirty enough, you're fireproof."

If that's what *you* want, you're almost there.
Just look at your neck and that gunk in your
    hair!
That's real insulation, I have to agree.
Shall we light up the blowtorch and see what
    we see?
Oh, you don't want to try yet? Then get in
    that tub
With this soap and this brush and this
    washcloth — and scrub!

Jerry

This is Jerry Jingle-Jangle
With his stockings all a-dangle
And his cowlick in a tangle.
He's a sight from any angle.

Mike (or Joe)

There is a boy I do not know
   Because we never met.
His name is Mike or maybe Joe
   Or maybe I forget.

Remembering is hardest when
   You never really knew
The thing you're thinking of. And yet
   Excuses will not do.

He has a name: everyone has.
   And if he has, I *should*
Remember what I think it was.
   I know my sister would.

She can remember on the spot
   What no one ever knew
Or ever heard about, or thought
   Could possibly be true.

The Flier

A young man in a hot-air balloon
Pulled the wrong rope and took off too soon —
   Too soon and too fast.
   He's back home in a cast,
And he has to be fed with a spoon.

Ode

The boy stood on the burning deck.
There on the deck stood he,
And everywhere beyond the flames
He thought he saw the sea.

It was indeed the sea he saw
Seesawing on the scene.
But most of all he seemed to see
The flames that seethed between.

He saw them seethe, he saw them saw
Between him and the sea.
And as he died he sang, or tried
To sing, "Oh Promise Me!"

That song he, sinking, sang, I say.
On treble sang it he.
But sad to add his voice went bad:
It cracked on the high sea.

Ah, sad to add his voice went bad
Though that was hardly strange,
For every cabin boy in time
Must suffer a C change.

The Man with Nothing to Say

There was a man with nothing to say,
   And no taste for keeping still.
"I like to listen to my own voice,"
   Said he, "And I think I will.

"If I had to wait for something to say,"
   Said he, "I would be so old
Before I got to make a speech,
   That everything would have been told

"A thousand times. Then who would come
   To listen and rejoice
At the nothing and all I have to say
   In my really remarkable voice?

"I can sound it high, I can sound it low,
   I can say 'Harumph!' so loud
It booms like a ton of TNT
   Set off in a thundercloud.

"I can whisper and hiss as soft as sleet
   When it falls on a silent sea.
I can tell a joke that has no point
   And chuckle so merrily

"That all who listen are so moved
    By my voice — so awfully awed
By my artistry, they look at me
    And no man dares applaud

"— For fear of course of breaking the spell
    Of the truly remarkable way
I fill the room with the boom-boom-boom
    Of my nothing whatever to say.

"With the whisper and hiss and tee-hee-hee
    And the ever-rising swell
of my boom-boom-boom as it fills the room
    With the nothing I tell so well."

And Now Kiddies — Captain Cuff!

Captain Cuff of the TV Rangers
Is hard on his friends and harder on strangers.
If he knows your sister and thinks she's sweet,
And you walk wrong on a one-way street
He'll shoot you once, and in the toe.
But if you're someone he doesn't know
And doesn't want to (he seldom does)
And he finds you asleep in the back of the bus
He'll empty his six-gun on your head
To wake you up to see if you're dead.

Better not answer. You might be right.
And he's never wrong. And he likes to fight.
He's a law man, awe man, quick-on-the-draw man,
Do-as-I-say and a give-me-no-jaw man.
He's Captain Cuff and he's rough and tough.
At five o'clock he does his stuff,
Because you like him. And since you do,
I have a question — what's wrong with you?

24

The Dragon Hunter

He drove into town with a ten-ton dragon
Lashed to the top of his old Volkswagen.
The head that is. About thirty feet
Of tail was dragging along the street.
He had tied a rusty roller skate
To the underside, but too much weight
Had squashed the wheels. Instead of turning
They threw off sparks like a gearbox burning.
He chugged and steamed and came to a stop
As his tires went pop! pop! and pop!
On Main in front of the barbershop.
Twenty-eight men came out for a look.
A TV crew raced up and took
A lot of pictures. He faced the crowd
Waving his arms and talking loud
And letting his tale stretch taller and taller,
And claiming a record. I'll bet a dollar
He was just putting on a show.
Did he suppose we didn't know
It was only a mangy old dinosaur?
— There aren't any dragons anymore!

It's Confusing

If a dove brought a letter in its beak,
And the postmark read "Sometime last week,"

Would it be from Jonah's whale, do you think?
That would mean it was written in octopus ink.

And I have to believe it would be so blurred
You couldn't make out a single word.

If you knew the language. Which, no doubt,
Whales do not speak as much as spout.

And even if it were from a whale,
Can you trust a dove to deliver the mail?

Since doves can't read, I have to guess
They never could find the right address.

Not that it matters. I'm just supposing.
But let me ask one question in closing:

Suppose it happened — where would you be?
The only answer is: All at sea.

The Seaside

We were strolling by the seaside.
    How glad I was we met.
I held her hand. She sweetly sighed,
    "My feet are getting wet."

My eyes were fixed on hers. Oh, ray
    Of love! Oh, golly gee!
I almost failed to hear her say,
    "It's halfway to my knee."

"Ah, joy," I sighed, "past knowing!"
    "Likewise, I'm sure," said she.
"But if you don't watch where we're going
    We may be lost at sea."

"At sea, on earth, or in the sky,
　I love you a pound and a peck."
"That *is* good measure, dear, but I
　Am in up to my neck!"

"What can it matter that the sea
　Rage, or the wild wind blow?"
Said she, "If you are asking me,
　My dear, I think I know!"

I felt her pull her hand away.
　I saw her form retreat.
A wave came rising out of the bay
　And knocked me off my feet.

I lost my love forever more,
　Oh, radiant and fair.
When you stroll along the shore,
　Remember there's water there.

The Diver

A hundred feet down in the sea
I saw sharks, and when they saw me,
   They said, "Let's have lunch."
   That's when I had a hunch
I was not in the right place to be.

When Jonah Sailed to Nineveh

When Jonah took an ocean trip
　His passage didn't cost a dime.
The captain threw him off the ship,
　But Jonah had a whale of a time.

The sea opened up for him.
　So did the whale's *glug-glug*.
His cabin in the whale was dim,
　A little bit slimy, but quite snug.

Three days and nights without a match
　To light a candle, Jonah sat,
While tons of fish slid down the hatch.
　A big one almost knocked him flat.

Three days and nights he groped about
　Slipping and sliding in the slime
Till the whale beached and burped him out.
　"Phew!" said Jonah. "It's about time!"

He picked a squid from one ear
　And sneezed a sardine from his nose.
"I'm saved!" said Jonah, "but I fear
　I do not smell quite like a rose."

"When this is written in the Bible,"
   Jonah thought, "I'll live in glory.
Though men of little faith are liable
   To think of it as a fish story."

But it's written down: I read it
   Word for word. And I tell you
Jonah was right there when he said it.
   Doesn't that prove it must be true?

He waded up the beach and found
   Some fishermen working on their gear.
They did not care to stay around.
   They raced off like a herd of deer

Holding their noses. Don't ask me
   How deer can run and hold their noses.
They left too fast for me to see.
   I heard them crying "Holy Moses!"

And, among other things, "Ee-yipe!
   It's hard to breathe!" They meant, I think,
That after three days fish turn ripe,
   And what they ripen to is — STINK.

Wading

I lost a shoe in a wave back there.
    I left it on the beach
While I was wading. I left it where
    No wave was supposed to reach.

But one came riding piggyback
    On another, and not the shore.
It came down with a terrible smack
    And back with a terrible roar.

And there I was with sand in my pants
    And seaweed in my eye,
And there's my shoe halfway to France
    While the laces wave good-bye.

And here I am, with a mile to go
    Over shells, and what shall I do?
— You'll have to go tenderfoot, tippy-toe.
    Next time bring an extra shoe.

Busy Is Better Than Nothing

Corkscrew eels are a curious sight
  As they corkscrew through the ocean.
Some corkscrew left. Some corkscrew right.
  Two kinds of perpetual motion.

They swim, of course, much faster than far.
  A mile around: one inch ahead.
Don't ask me why. That's how things are
  With corkscrew eels. As I have said,

They're a curious sight. If you watch too long
  You may find that you get dizzy.
But you must admit that, right or wrong,
  Corkscrew eels keep very busy.

They don't do much but they do it hard.
  They practice day and practice night.
They corkscrew inch by foot by yard.
  Some to the left. Some to the right.

Foot by yard by rod by mile,
  Around and around and around they go.
And every once in a little while
  They move ahead an inch or so.

It isn't much, I must agree.
   But even a bit of an inch or so
Is better than nothing. Especially
   When you don't have anywhere to go.

So don't be idle. Find something to do,
   If what you do isn't real,
It's better than nothing. I think that's true
   — If you're a corkscrew eel.

How to Assemble a Toy

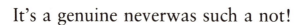

This is the whatsit that fits on the knob
Of the gadget that turns the thingamabob.
This is the dingus that fits in place
With the doodad next to the whosiface.
This is the jigger that goes in the hole
Where the gizmo turns the rigamarole.
Now slip the ding-dang into the slot
Of the jugamalug, and what have you got?

It's a genuine neverwas such a not!

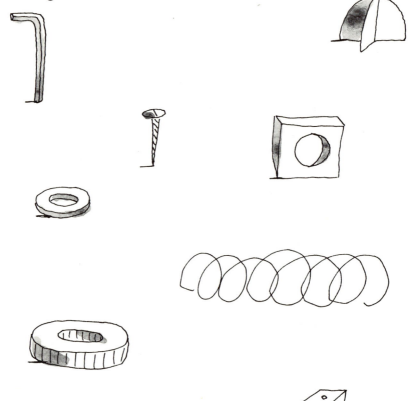

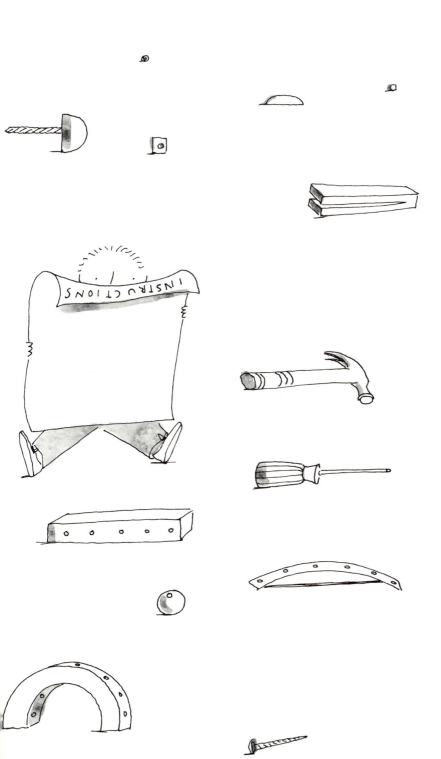

INSTRUCTIONS

The Mechanic

You must admit I had to be smart
To take a grandfather clock apart.

You certainly are a crackerjack!
Are you smart enough to put it back?
I mean with all the pieces in place
And the face in front and the hands
    on the face
And the ticks on the tocks and
    the tocks on the ticks.
Dad will be coming home at six.
That's just about now. And he just might
Decide it wasn't exactly bright
To scatter those pieces all over the floor.
What are those things by the closet door?
Just extra parts? Well, good enough.
But don't blame me if Dad gets rough.
Smart? He'll know how to make you smart.
And I can guess where he's going to start.
Uh-oh! I hear his car in the drive.
I'll bet he's going to skin you alive!
Here, take this towel. Your one last chance
Is to stuff it into the seat of your pants!

A Wise One Knows His Nose

The bulldog's snout is flat in its face.
    The collie's sticks out far.
These are the basic facts of the case.
    Depending on which you are

And on how you feel about window fans
    And breezes up your nose,
You may choose what's wise for your shape
      and size —
    Well back, or right up close.

It's what we do and how we do it
    That measures our success.
Be sure about the length of your snout.
    Don't settle for a guess.

Our deeds, it's true, reach far beyond
    The best the doer knows.
But every beast should see at least
    As far as the end of his nose.

A Panda Is a Teddy Bear

A panda is a teddy bear
That came out black except for the white.
It lives too far from everywhere
To know it isn't colored right.

The panda doesn't think it's far
From where it lives. But if you get
That far, ask someone where you are.
You'll be told "China" or "Tibet."

That's far enough from anywhere
A teddy bear would care to go,
That if it met a panda there
It really wouldn't care to know

Quite where it was. And couldn't tell,
Because the signposts nailed to trees
Would not explain it very well,
Being written in Chinese.

And so the panda doesn't know
It looks like a mixed-up teddy bear.
And if you tried to tell it so,
You'd find it really wouldn't care.

The Early Bird

The early bird — so I have read —
Gets the worm. I stay in bed
And put myself in the worm's shoes.
Had it stayed in for one more snooze
And then a second, then a third,
By then, would not the early bird
Have gone to feed the early cat?
I take a worm's eye view of that.
Why get up early just to start
The day as bird food? Call that smart?
Ask any worm and it will say,
"Being eaten spoils my day!"
Getting out of bed too soon
Spoils mine. Call me at noon.

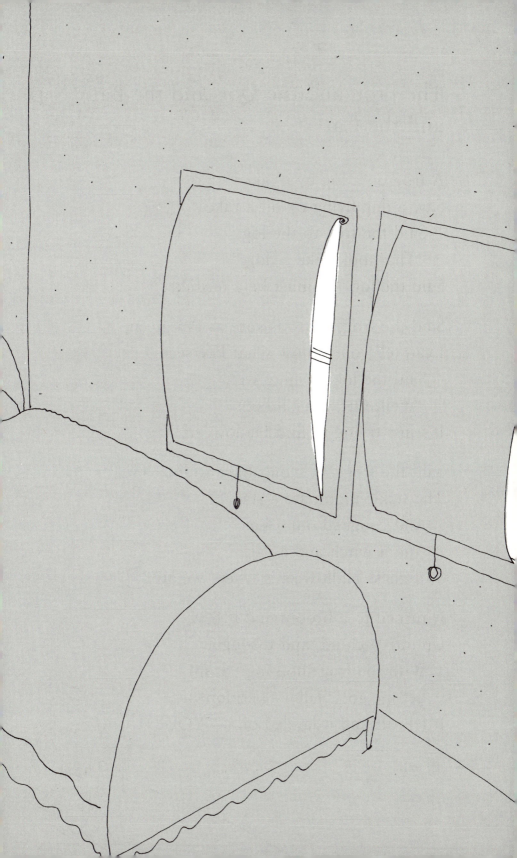

The Frog and the Dog and the Bat and the Cat

A frog on a log by a lake
Saw a dog flying by on a rake.
   Said the frog to the log,
   "That looks like a dog."
Said the log, "It must be a mistake."

Said the frog, "Just as sure as I'm green,
I can tell you I know what I've seen."
   Said the log, turning wet,
   "Well, OK, but I'll bet
It's just trying to find Halloween."

Said the frog, "It won't have to look far.
The sickle moon ate a star
   And coughed out a bat
   And a witch and a cat.
So I guess Halloween's where we are."

It turned to a broom and it flew
Up into a cloud, and through,
   With the frog shouting "Stop!
   Let me go!" Till — kerplop! —
It fell off and it landed on — YOU!

A Dividend Opinion

Said the Aliquant to the Aliquot,
"You're all used up, and I am not."
"Used up?" said the Aliquot. "Not a bit.
I happen to be a perfect fit.
You're a raveled thread. A wrong number.
You're about as useful as scrap lumber.
I slip into place like a mitered joint.
You hang out over your decimal point
Like a monkey asquat in a cuckoo's nest
With your tail adangle, self-impressed
By the way you twitch the thing about.
Stuck up about nothing but sticking out.
If I'm used up, you will discover
You're no fresh start. You're just left over
From nothing anyone would want,"
Said the Aliquot to the Aliquant.

The Wind

The morning after the night before,
   The wind came in when I opened the door.
It blew the "Welcome" off the mat.
   It blew the fur right off my cat.
It blew my shirttail out of my pants.
   It grabbed the curtains and started to dance
Around and around and around about
   Till I opened a window and kicked it out.

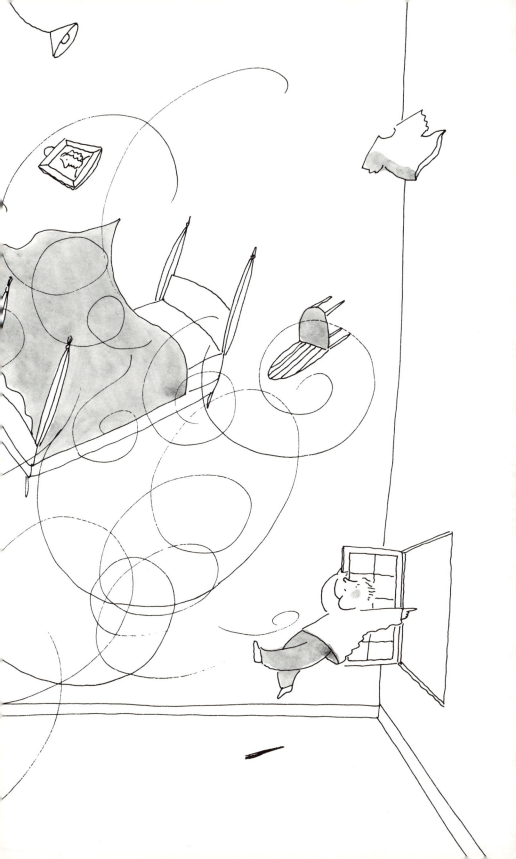